A Special Gift

for

_____

from

_____

date

_____

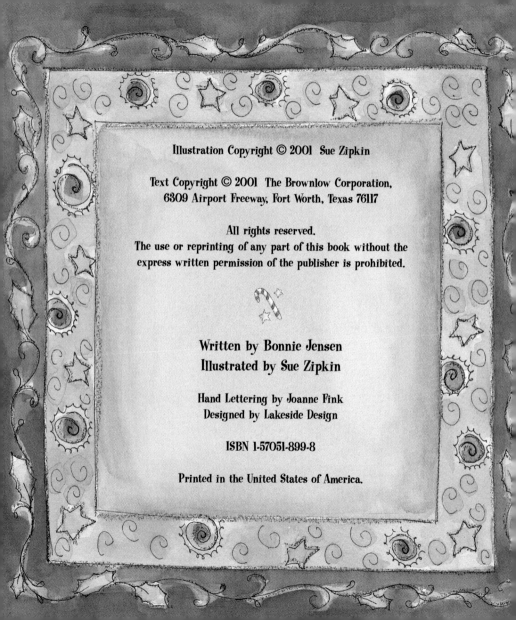

Written by Bonnie Jensen
Illustrated by Sue Zipkin

Hand Lettering by Joanne Fink
Designed by Lakeside Design

ISBN 1-57051-899-8

Have a Holly Jolly CHRISTMAS

Written by Bonnie Jensen
Illustrated by Sue Zipkin

Brownlow

Introduction

The warmth of friends and family,
the light in a child's eyes, festive decorations,
and twinkling lights are all a part of the
excitement and wonder of the Christmas season.
Nothing else brings out the good in people
quite like Christmas. Whether it's leaving a gift for
your postal carrier or putting a wreath on your car,
there are so many little things you can do
to give another person a reason to smile.

This little book contains a lot of ideas
to help you spread good cheer to others,
but feel free to experiment
and add your own variations to the list.

So go on now and have yourself a
HOLLY JOLLY CHRISTMAS!

Fill your mailbox with candy
for the mail carrier on Christmas Eve.
Bundle it up so it's easy to remove
and don't forget to add
a thankful-for-you note.

HOLLY JOLLY VARIATION:

If you know your mail carrier's schedule,
make sure to peek out the window
when they discover your sweet surprise.
Watching someone's face
light up is incredibly festive.

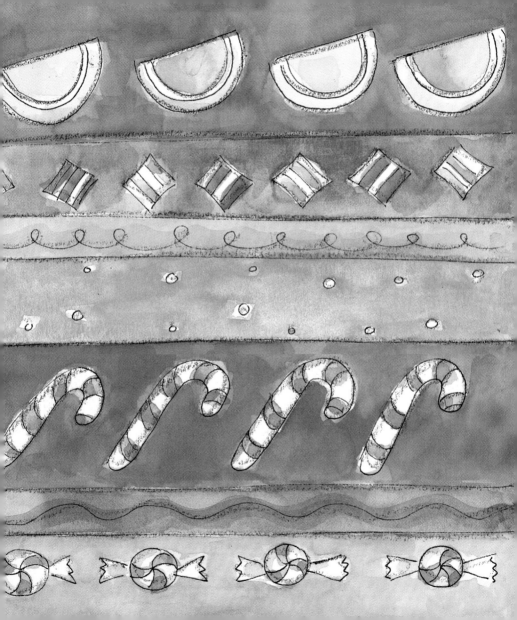

Be a good neighbor. Make a hot chocolate mix
or bake them a little something
and deliver it with a big smile.

Holly Jolly Variation:

Go the extra mile and add a coupon
for one lawn mowing or leaf raking
during the appropriate season—
redeemable on the day of their choice.

Easy Homemade Hot Cocoa Mix:

2 cups instant nonfat dry milk powder
2 cups miniature marshmallows
1 cup powdered nondairy creamer
1 cup semisweet chocolate chips
1 cup unsweetened cocoa

Stir all ingredients together until thoroughly blended.
Pour the mix into a clear jar
and tie a festive silk ribbon around the top.

Volunteer to read for children at
your local library during the holiday season.
Choose your favorite Christmas book
or share a story from your childhood memories.

Holly Jolly Variation:

Bring a red sack filled with Christmas cookies
or candy to hand out to the children
after they've been quiet
and attentive for story time.

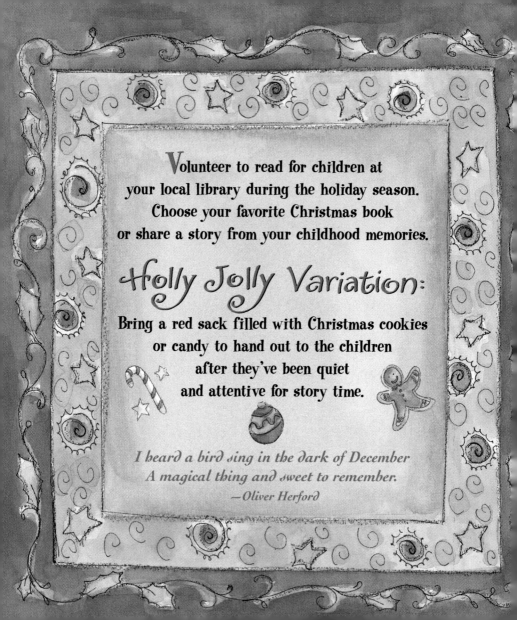

I heard a bird sing in the dark of December
A magical thing and sweet to remember.
—Oliver Herford

Leave anonymous "Happy Holiday" notes
for family, friends, or co-workers.
Include a compliment or
word of encouragement in each one
to make them feel special.

HOLLY JOLLY VARIATION:

Think about adding more than words
to your anonymous notes—
like dollar bills, candy,
or gift certificates for movie rentals.

At Christmas
play and make
good cheer.

For Christmas comes
but once a year!

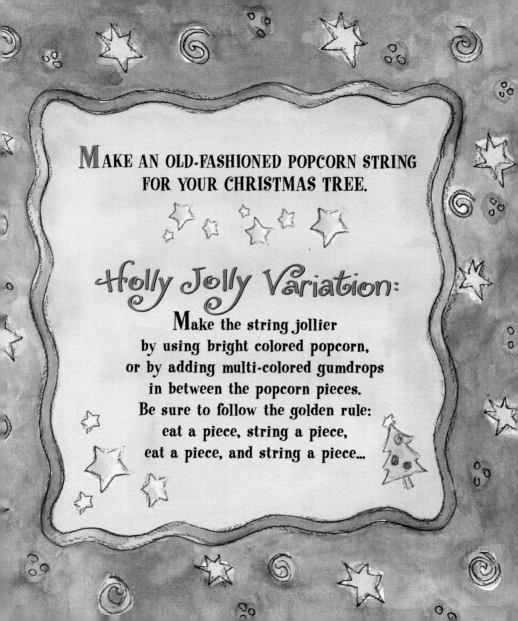

MAKE AN OLD-FASHIONED POPCORN STRING
FOR YOUR **C**HRISTMAS TREE.

Holly Jolly Variation:

Make the string jollier
by using bright colored popcorn,
or by adding multi-colored gumdrops
in between the popcorn pieces.
Be sure to follow the golden rule:
eat a piece, string a piece,
eat a piece, and string a piece...

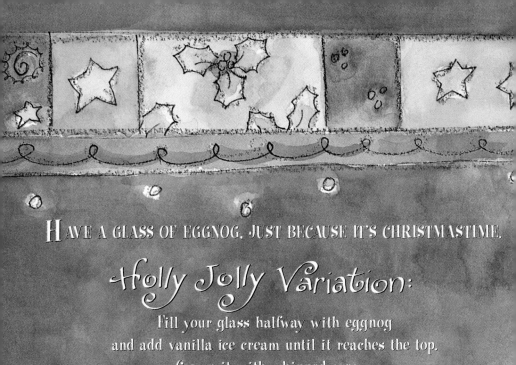

Have a glass of eggnog, just because it's Christmastime.

Holly Jolly Variation:

Fill your glass halfway with eggnog
and add vanilla ice cream until it reaches the top.
Crown it with whipped cream.
Try to remember why you ever avoided this holiday treat.

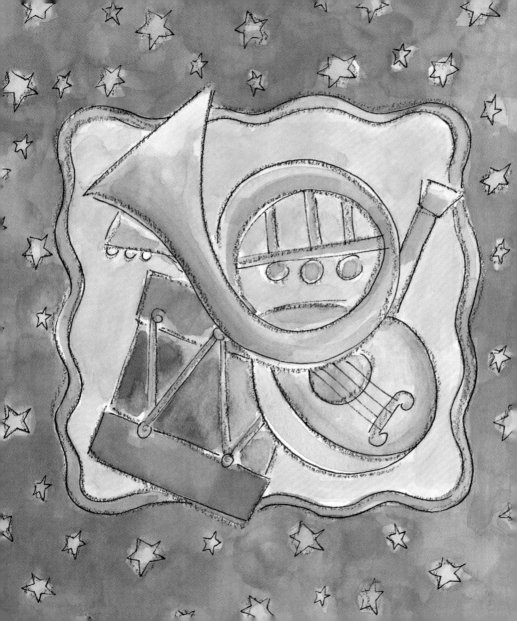

Treat yourself, with friends and family,
to a local Christmas production.
No grand scale needed here—
some of the most touching performances
can be found in small venues.

HOLLY JOLLY VARIATION:

Volunteer to be part of a local Christmas production.
Have fun with it and let it be a gentle reminder
that being a blessing to others
is the best gift of all.

Start a snowball fight. No snow?
Start a water fight and remind everyone that it
is the liquid form of snow.

Holly Jolly Variation:

A pillow fight
will do in a pinch.
Avoid fireplaces and Christmas trees.
Make it more festive
by using those decorative little
Christmas pillows.

LET IT SNOW!
LET IT SNOW!
LET IT SNOW!

GO ICE-SKATING.

Be it rink, pond, or lake,
there's bound to be someplace you can go
to take part in this wintry activity.

HOLLY JOLLY VARIATION:

Take a whole bunch of children along
(or adults who are willing to act like children).
Lots of laughter and falling down
adds to the overall joy of the experience.

*I have come that they might have life,
and that they might
have it more abundantly.*
John 10:10

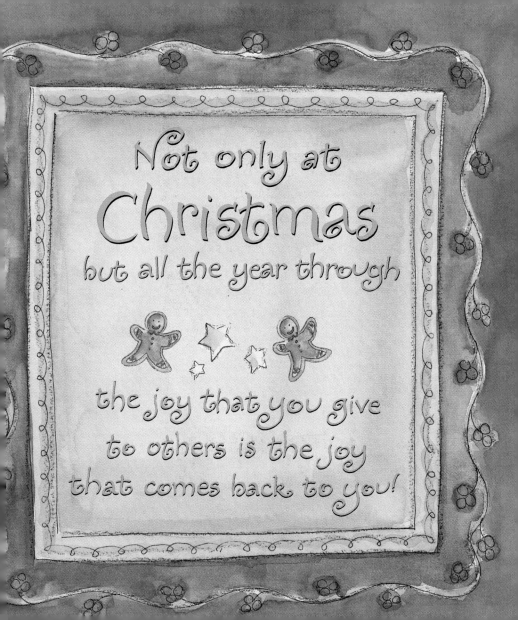

Not only at
Christmas
but all the year through

the joy that you give
to others is the joy
that comes back to you!

REPLACE THE CANDY JAR IN YOUR OFFICE
WITH A COOKIE JAR FOR THE HOLIDAY SEASON.

Holly Jolly Variation:

Invite everyone in the office
to take turns filling the cookie jar with
their own special Christmas baked goods.

I always smile when I see
a snowman standing in a yard.
There is definite charm in the array of things
chosen from the eyes, nose, mouth, and arms.
With or without buttons and a scarf,
they're adorned beautifully with things unseen—
memories— laughter— loving kindness— simple joy.

Call a senior care center in your community
to get a list of residents
who don't receive mail on a regular basis.
Send them each a Christmas card.

HOLLY JOLLY VARIATION:

Hand-deliver the cards,
get to know one or two residents,
and begin a friendship that will enrich your life.

Glory to God in the highest,
and on earth peace,
goodwill to men.
—Luke 2:14

MAKE PAPER SNOWFLAKES.
Fold a letter-size sheet into quarters
and cut out every shape you can think of.
OPEN. VOILA! A SNOWFLAKE.

Holly Jolly Variation:

Display your handiwork
on a desktop Christmas tree
and add some Styrofoam snowballs
to complete the ensemble.

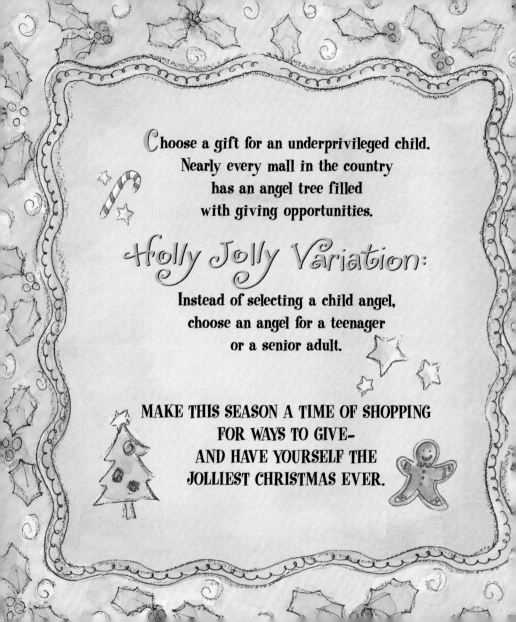

Choose a gift for an underprivileged child.
Nearly every mall in the country
has an angel tree filled
with giving opportunities.

Holly Jolly Variation:

Instead of selecting a child angel,
choose an angel for a teenager
or a senior adult.

**MAKE THIS SEASON A TIME OF SHOPPING
FOR WAYS TO GIVE—
AND HAVE YOURSELF THE
JOLLIEST CHRISTMAS EVER.**

The heart of
the giver
makes the gift
dear and
precious.

— MARTIN LUTHER

VISIT A TOY STORE.
See if your favorite childhood toy
is still being made,
no matter how strange it might appear
in its modern form.

Holly Jolly Variation:

To help see the wonder of Christmas
through a child's eyes,
take a child with you to a toy store
and help them shop for a friend,
a relative, or a needy child.

Throw a
"KICK-OFF THE CHRISTMAS SEASON"
party for your family and friends.
Watch a classic holiday cartoon
and follow it with "It's a Wonderful Life"
or any other heartwarming movie of your choice.
Serve popcorn, peanuts, cookies, and hot cocoa.

Holly Jolly Variation:

GO ON A BRIEF CAROLING EXPEDITION
TO YOUR NEIGHBORS-
THEN INVITE THEM TO THE PARTY!

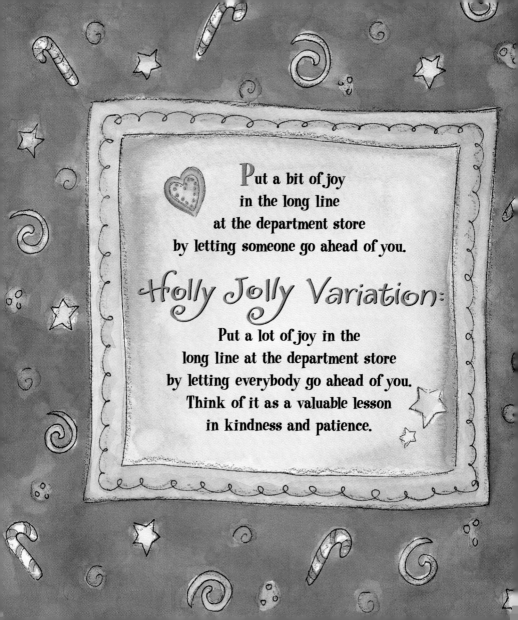

P ut a bit of joy
in the long line
at the department store
by letting someone go ahead of you.

Holly Jolly Variation:

Put a lot of joy in the
long line at the department store
by letting everybody go ahead of you.
Think of it as a valuable lesson
in kindness and patience.

Decorate Your Car!

Tie a wreath to the front, put ribbons on the antenna,
or hang mistletoe from the rearview mirror...

Holly Jolly Variation:

Line the back window with battery-operated lights
or a garland, or put window adhesive cutouts here and there.
Be sure and play Christmas music
as you go on all your errands.

For everything there is a season,
and a time to every purpose under the heaven.
—Ecclesiastes 3:1 KJV

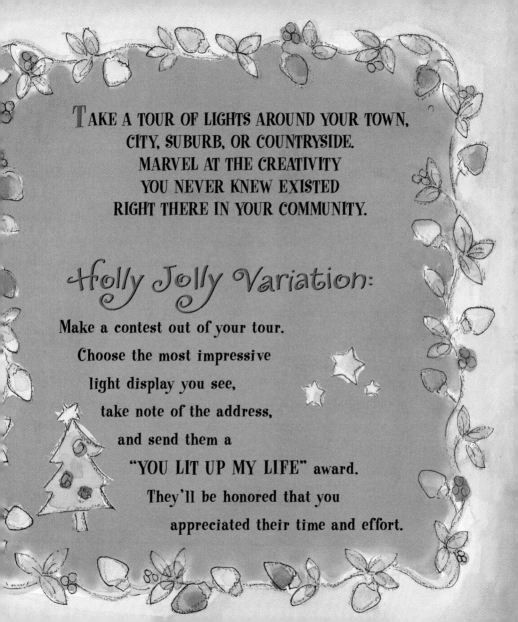

TAKE A TOUR OF LIGHTS AROUND YOUR TOWN,
CITY, SUBURB, OR COUNTRYSIDE.
MARVEL AT THE CREATIVITY
YOU NEVER KNEW EXISTED
RIGHT THERE IN YOUR COMMUNITY.

Holly Jolly Variation:

Make a contest out of your tour.
Choose the most impressive
light display you see,
take note of the address,
and send them a
"YOU LIT UP MY LIFE" award.
They'll be honored that you
appreciated their time and effort.

At Christmas
all people
smile in the
same language.

Make a Christmas frame ornament,
insert your picture,
and give it to your mom.

Holly Jolly Variation:

GIVE YOUR MOM SOME EXTRA HUGS
this Christmas and tell her
you'll never outgrow the joy
of having the best mom in the world.

Her children arise and call her blessed.
Proverbs 31:28

Colusa County Free Library

738 Market Street
Colusa, CA 95932
Phone: 458-7671

CUP